Once Upon A Wish

A holiday collection and more...

Emily Bear

pianist & composer

www.emilybear.com

Jordan King Music USA

P.O. Box 271, Rockford, IL 61105

ISBN 0982601518

Table of Contents

The ASCAP Foundation Awards

Once Upon A Wish was composed
by 7 year old Emily Bear. A beautiful follow-up to
her second CD, *"The Love In Us"*, the songs showcase her
versatile styles and ability to touch the listener with her musical
emotions. Debuted on The Ellen Degeneres Show, the title song,
"Once Upon a Wish", was written as a wedding gift for Ellen.
"Christmas Bells" and *"Giving"* are a tribute to the holiday season.
Emily's music has a worldwide emotional appeal that
seems to speak from her heart to ours.

———•———

ᦥ *Performance Highlights** ᦥ

Performed a solo concert at **The White House.**

Appeared on **The Ellen Degeneres Show** four times!

Made her orchestral debut performing her original song,
"The Love In Us", with members of the **Orlando Symphony Orchestra.**

Debuted at the **Ravinia Music Festival** at age 5, the youngest
soloist in the festival's more than 100 year history. Emily was invited
back to Ravinia for another solo concert the following year, where she
performed again for a capacity audience.

Recipient of a **2008 ASCAP Morton Gould Young Composer
Competition Award** for her original song, *"Northern Lights"*.

Featured in the premier episode of **"All You Need Is Music"**
– A new **PBS television show.**

Opened the 2007 **Chicago Thanksgiving Day Parade.**

ᦥ ᦥ

Dedicated to using her talent to help and inspire others,
Emily is donating a portion of the proceeds from the sale of
"Once Upon A Wish" songbooks and CDs to the
Ronald McDonald House Charities.

Giving

Music by
EMILY BEAR

Andante (♩ = ca. 63)

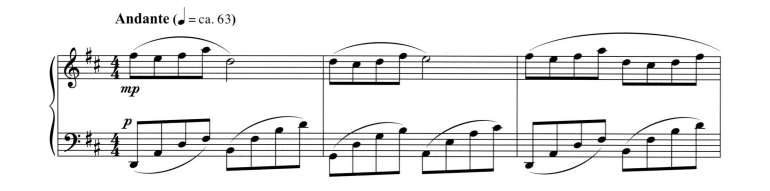

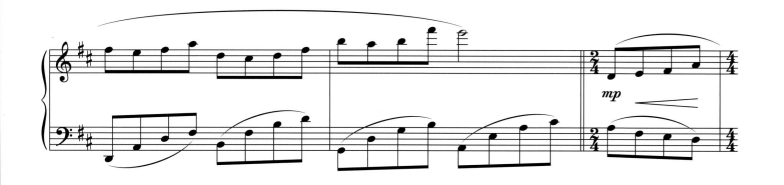

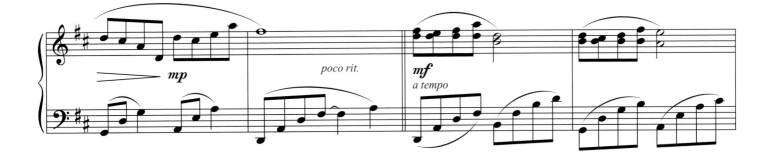

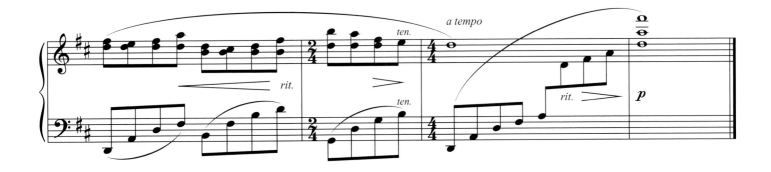

Lillian's Love

Music by
EMILY BEAR

Moderato (♩ = ca. 60)

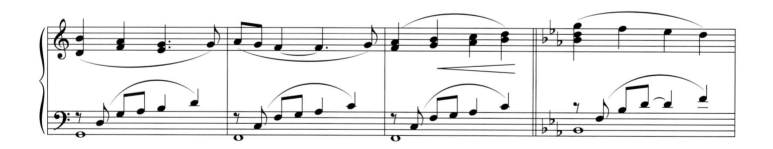

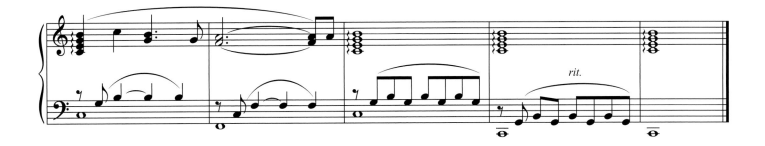

Wyndham Court

Music by
EMILY BEAR

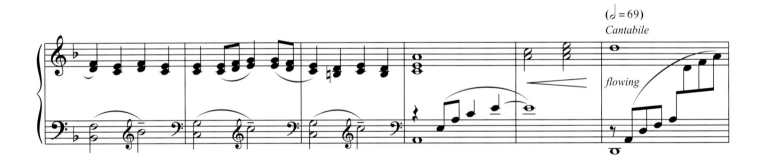

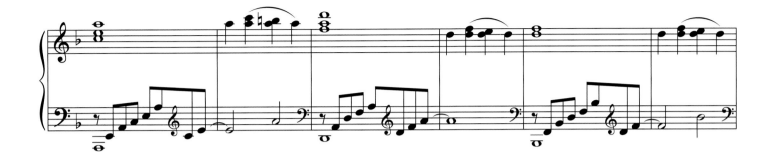

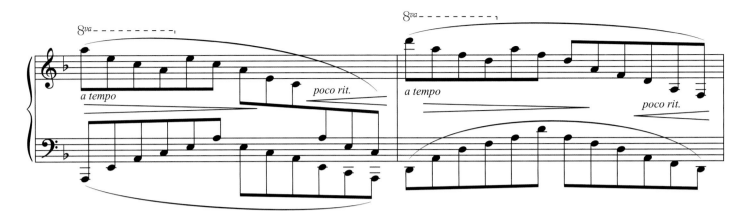

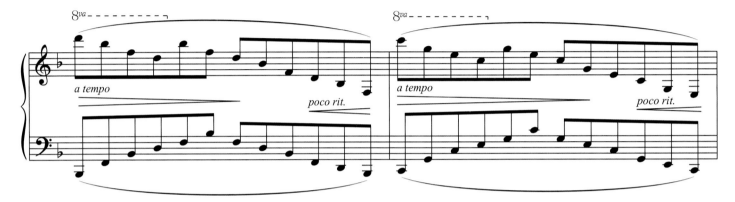

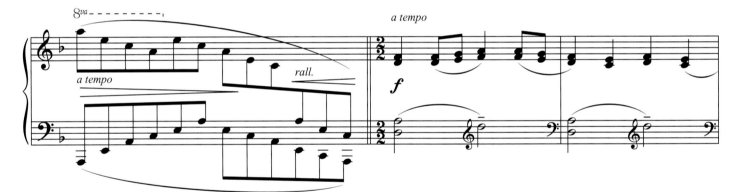

Motherlove

Music by
EMILY BEAR

Adagio (♩ = ca. 60)

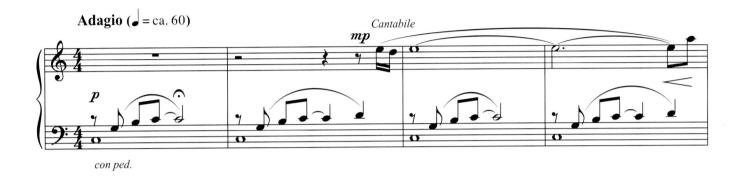

con ped.

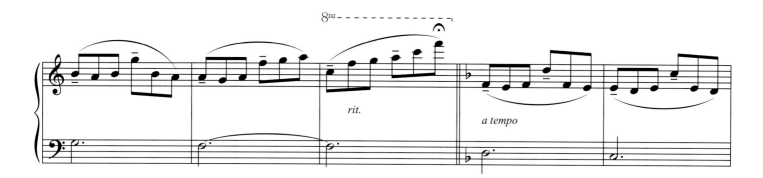

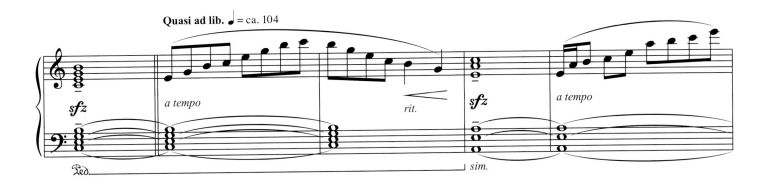

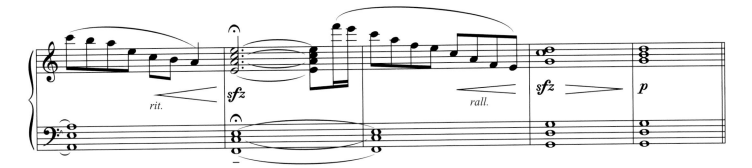

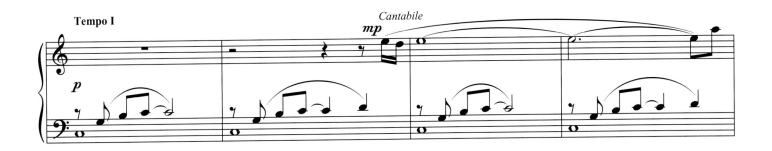

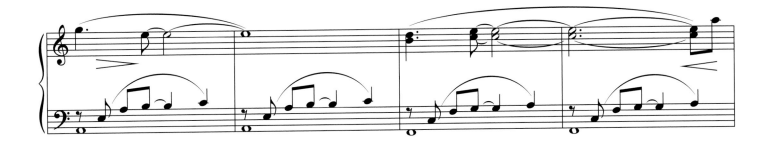

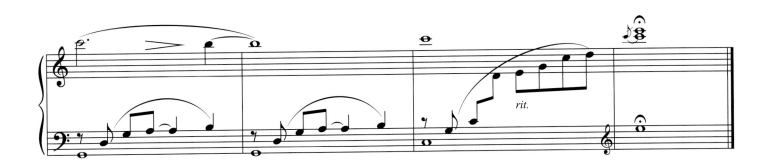

Out of Control

Music by
EMILY BEAR

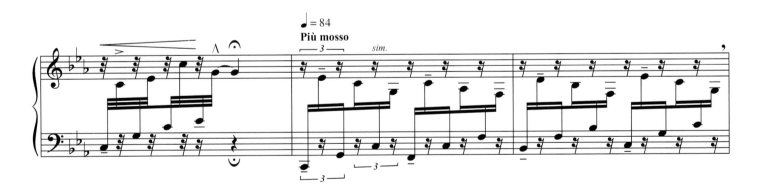

Tempo I

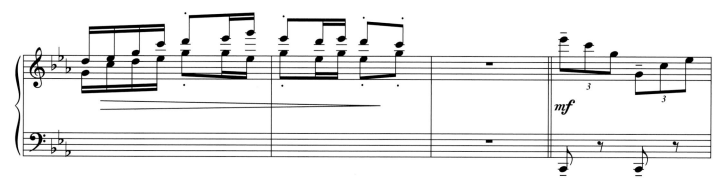

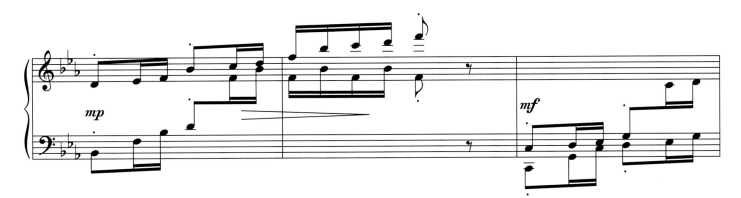

Flamengo

Music by
EMILY BEAR

Allegro (♩ = ca. 120)

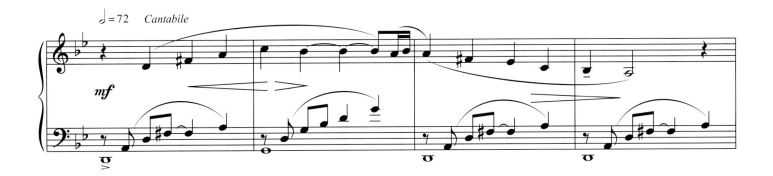

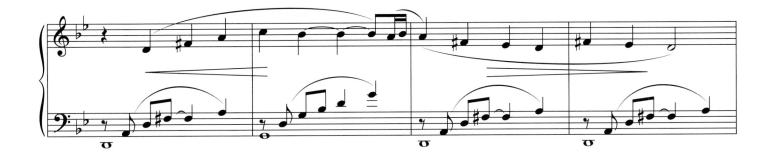

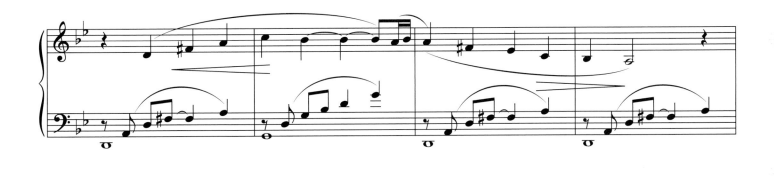

Rubato

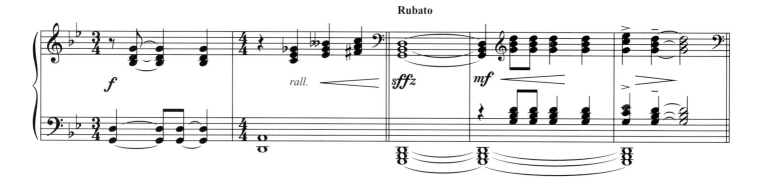

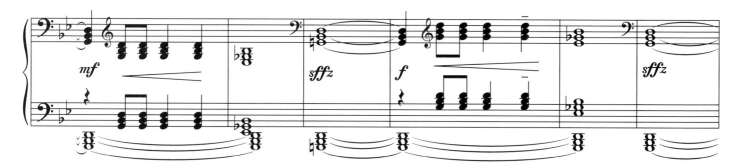

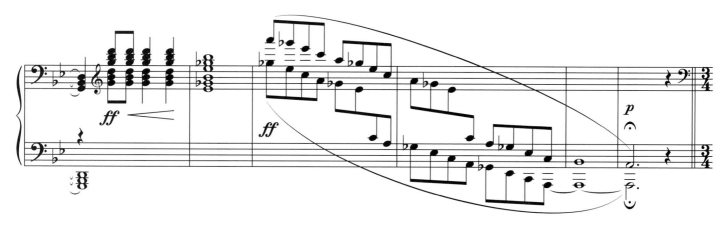

Tempo I

Christmas Bells

Music by
EMILY BEAR

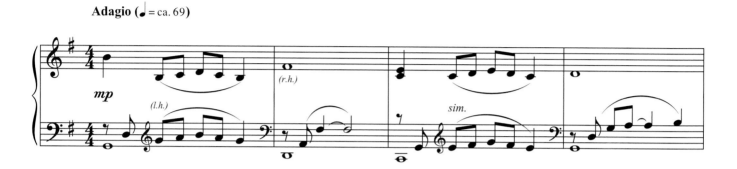

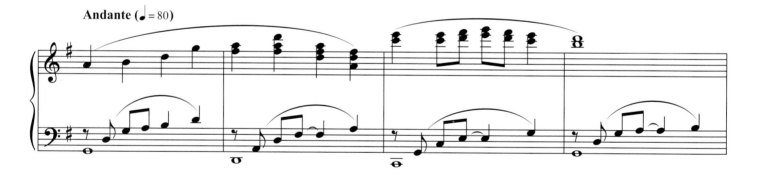

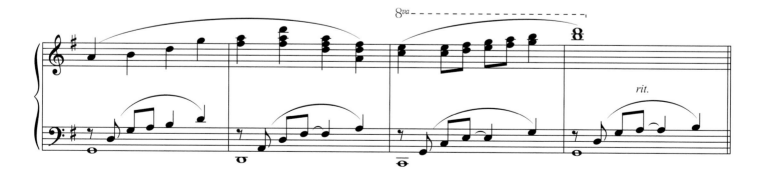

a tempo

Adagio ($\bullet$ = ca. 69)

Once Upon A Wish

Music by
EMILY BEAR

Rubato, quasi ad lib.

Allegro (♩ = ca. 120) **Più mosso** (♩ = 138)

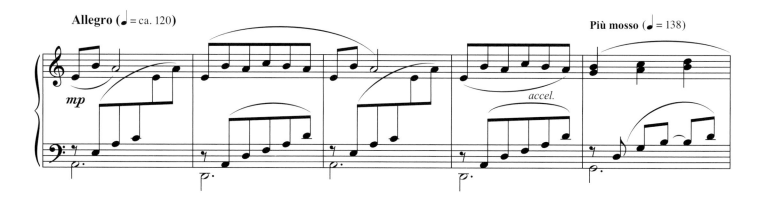

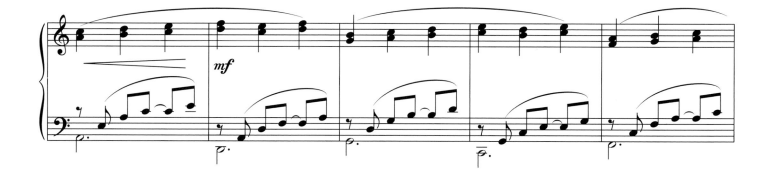

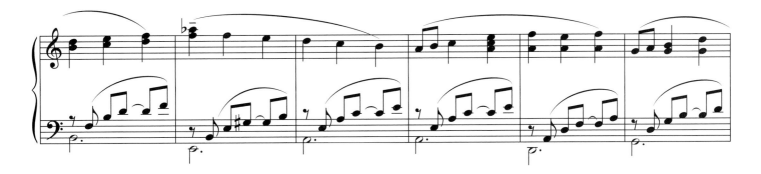

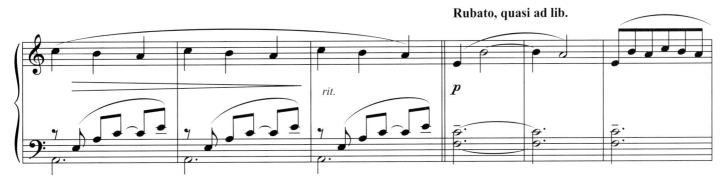

Rubato, quasi ad lib.

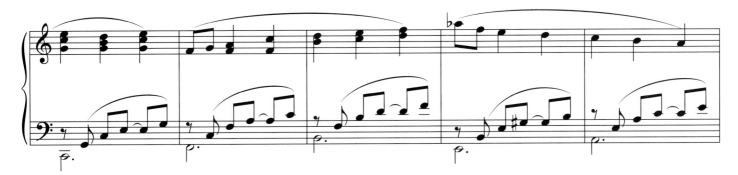

Meno mosso

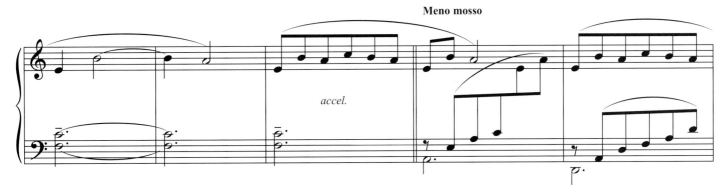

Mary's Hope

Music by
EMILY BEAR

Gently with expression ($\bullet$ = ca. 88)

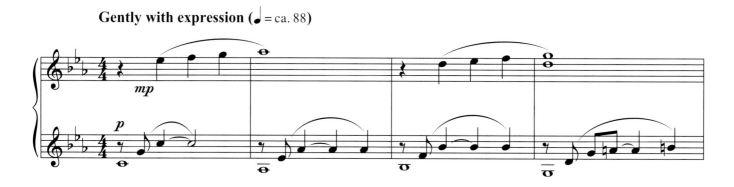

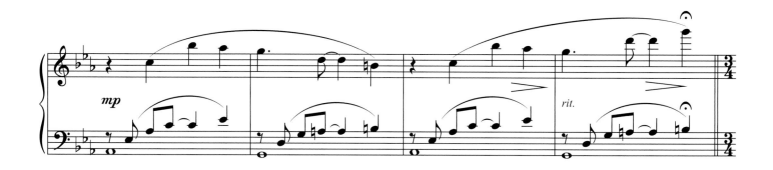

Più mosso ($\bullet$. = 48)

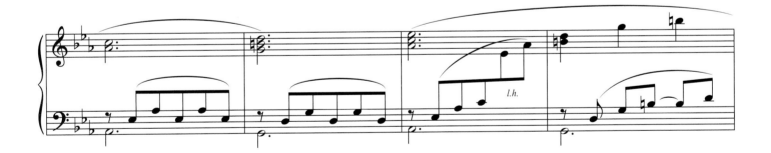

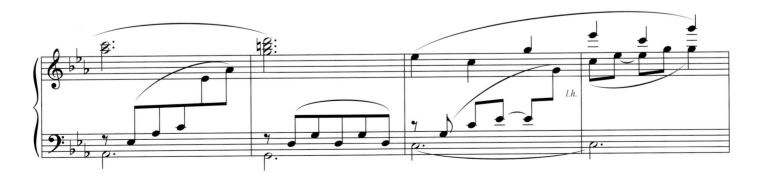

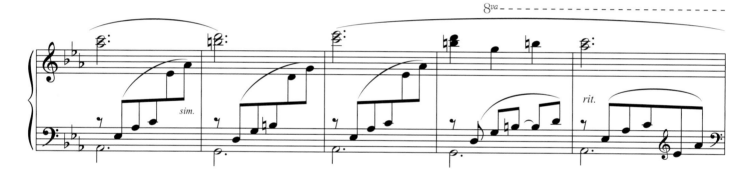

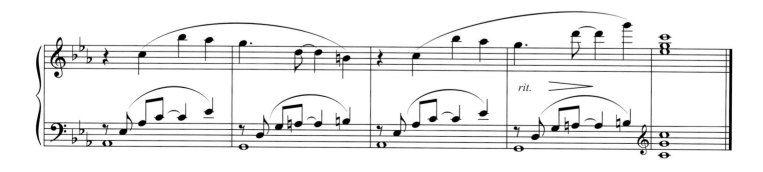

Aspen

Music by
EMILY BEAR

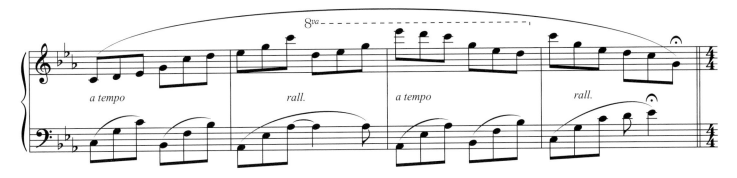

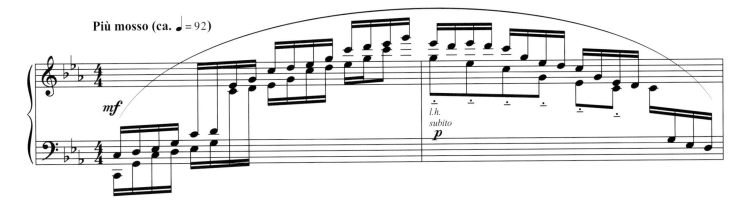

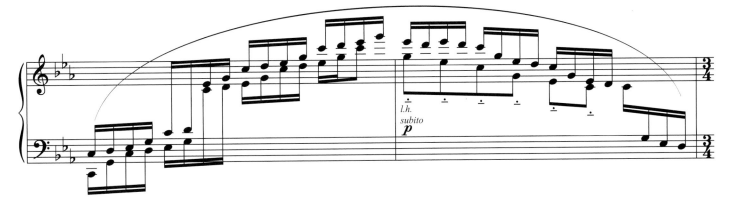

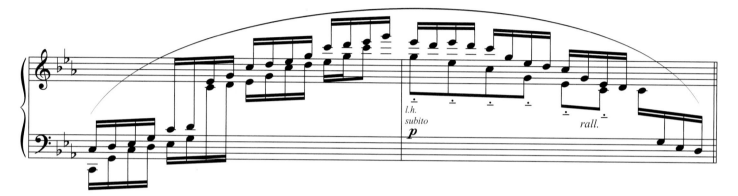

Meno mosso (♩ = 76)

Tempo I (♩ = 92)

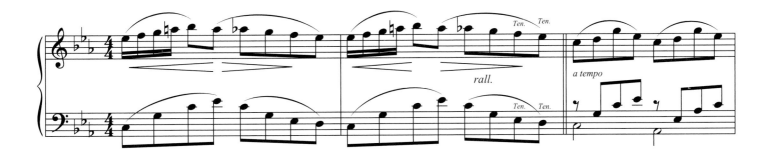

Rubato sostenuto (♩. = 46)

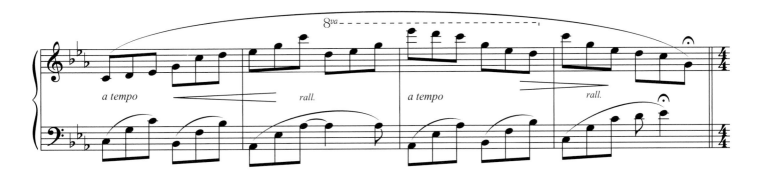

Più mosso (ca. ♩ = 88)

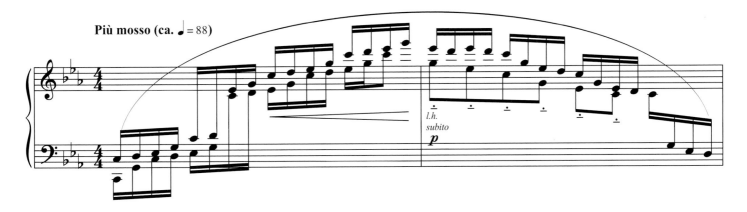

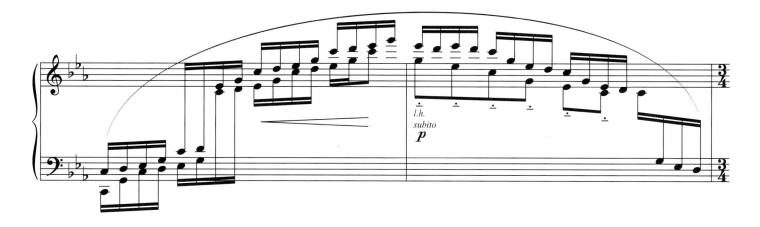

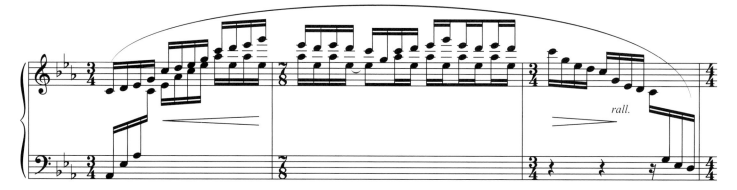

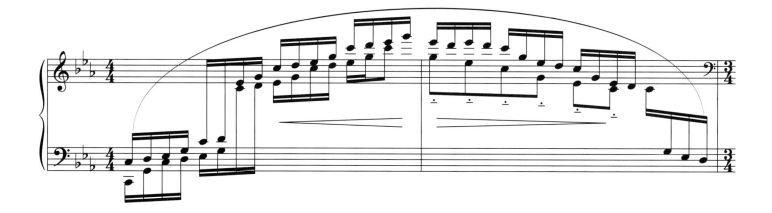

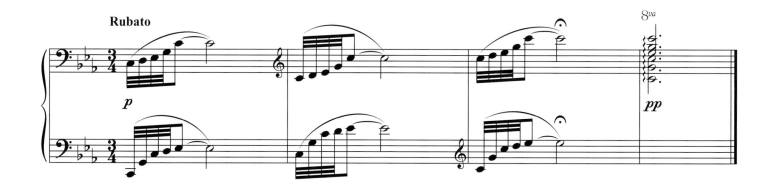

34

Once Upon A Wish

A holiday collection and more...

A musical collection inspired by nature, emotions,

and relationships - given a voice though music.

From wind whispering through the leaves

of the aspen trees, to the tenderness of a mother

holding her sleeping newborn, a tribute to a

beautiful life lived, or an English Tudor castle,

Emily paints pictures with her music -

touching our hearts.

Book Design by: Bill Edmundson and Andrea Bear

Photos by: Andrea Bear, George May

www.emilybear.com